The Statler Brothers

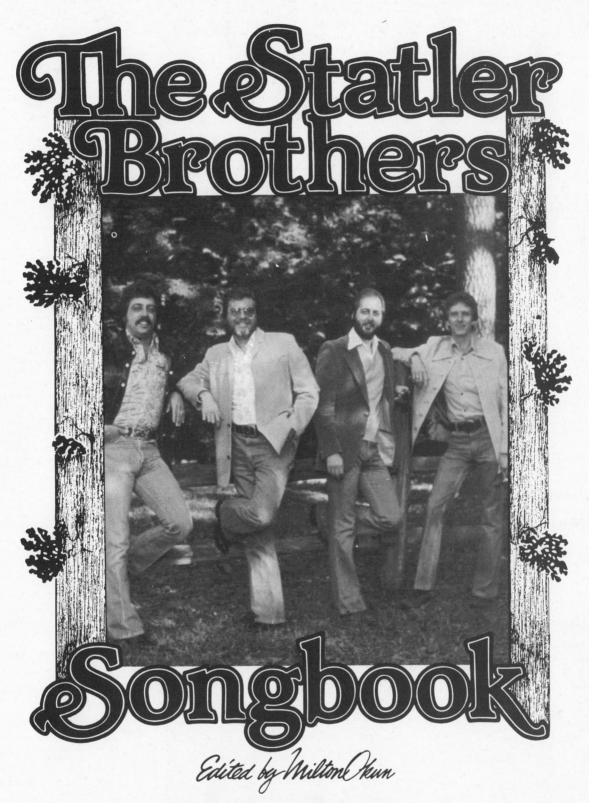

Songbook

Edited by Milton Okun

Associate Music Editor   Dan Fox
Art Director   Gil Gjersvik

ISBN 0-89524-044-0

The Statler Brothers

Songbook

Recently named the International Group of the Year, and performing to SRO crowds in cities across the nation where they broke all time attendance records, the Statler Brothers continue to climb the charts year after year. For six years in a row they have been presented with the Country Music Association's Best Vocal Group Award.

As boyhood friends in their home town of Staunton, Virginia, the Statler Brothers were first inspired by the music of two white gospel groups, The Blackwood Brothers and The Statesmen. They carried the gospel sound into country music in 1964, hosting their own television program in Virginia. During one of their appearances, they were seen by Johnny Cash who made them part of his touring show. A recording contract followed and their unique style of music swept the nation.

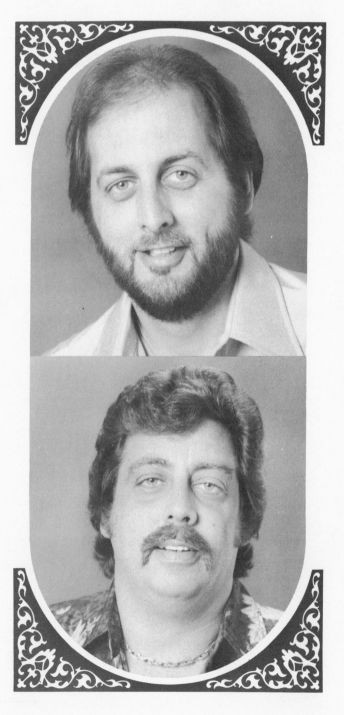

Don Reid

The lead singer of the Statler Brothers is Don Reid. He does most of the writing for the group, but gives full credit to the others for help in working out the songs. Born on June 5, 1945 in Staunton, Virginia, Don has a wife Gloria, and two sons, D (age 10) and Langdon (age 3). When he isn't singing, his hobbies include old films, especially cowboy movies, mysteries and comedies.

Harold Reid

Harold Reid, Don's brother, sings bass for the ensemble. Born on August 21, 1939, Harold has a wife Brenda, and five children, Kim, Karmen, Kodi, Kasey, and Wil. Although very modest about his own abilities, he has helped write some of the Statler Brothers' biggest hits including Class of '57 and Do You Know You Are My Sunshine. Harold feels very lucky to be able to do what he likes for a living and considers the gospel style easier than other quartet styles such as barbershop.

The harmony of the Statler Brothers is evident, not only in their music but in their personal lives as well. Their enduring personal friendship is the key to the solidarity and longevity of the group. They take care of one another, know when to come on and when to leave each other alone. They greatly appreciate the awards, fame and publicity bestowed upon them, but most importantly, they value the people in their audiences.

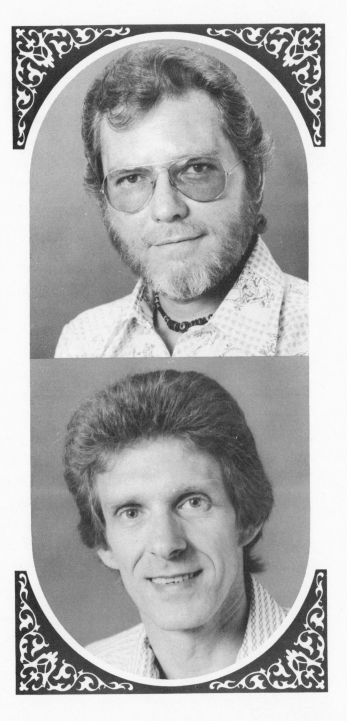

Lew DeWitt

The Statler Brothers' tenor is Lew DeWitt. Inspired by Bill Kenny (lead singer of the Inkspots), and Denver Dale Crumpler (tenor with The Statesmen), Lew does some writing for the group (he composed their first crossover hit Flowers On The Wall*), as well as playing guitar on stage. He was born on March 12, 1938, and lives in Staunton with his wife Joyce Ann, four children, two stepdaughters, and a dog named Dorothy.*

Phil Balsley

Phil Balsley sings baritone for the group, although he occasionally sings lead. He was introduced to quartet sounds in the early 50's by a local group, and gradually adapted the white gospel sound to country music. Among his favorite groups are The Blackwoods, The Statesmen, and the Rangers Quartet. Phil was born on August 8, 1939, has a wife Wilma, and three children, Greg (age 15), Mark (age 14), and Leah (age 10). He would like the group to become more involved with T.V., while maintaining artistic control of the production.

Performance Notes

The style of the Statler Brothers, being essentially vocal, is not an easy one to capture on paper. What we have tried to do is make their style playable on piano and guitar in a practical and fairly easy way without sacrificing much of its subtle country flavor. We'd like to tell you, though, that any arrangement on paper is an approximation of what's on the record, and the charts in this book should be regarded as blueprints to build on rather than something to be followed with mechanical precision.

We have used small grace notes to suggest the many vocal embellishments used by the Statlers. These, however, are to be sung only, and not played on piano.

For example, this bar from "New York City" (page 74) *

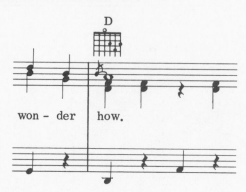

is played without the grace note

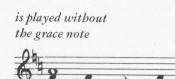

won – der how.

but sung (more or less)

how_____

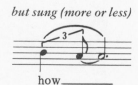

Guitar → D
(Capo up 1 fret)

Piano → Eb

A7
Bb7

(from "Pictures" page 75) *

pic – ture that__ we took__ in Cin – cin – nat – i _____ The

The Statler Brothers' usual voicing, derived from their gospel roots, is (starting at the top) Tenor, Lead, Baritone, Bass. In order to keep the melody in the clear, we have made sure it is always the highest note in the right hand unless otherwise indicated. Whenever practical, the tenor is dropped an octave and added in the accompaniment as a lower voice.

Guitarists will appreciate the care we have taken with chord diagrams. Each chord diagram has been individually engraved, not pre-printed and pasted in. This allows us to use many unusual chords and to give the most appropriate fingering for the common chords.

All the arrangements are presented in the original recorded key (except where indicated). Where this is awkward for the guitar, we have included a double set of chord symbols. The lower set (in Roman face type) indicates the chords for the piano; the upper set (in Italic face) and the diagrams give the chords for guitar. Appropriate capo instructions allow the guitarist to play along with the record or with the piano. (see example above)

Occasionally the D tuning is called for. This means that the 6th string of the guitar is lowered a full step to D. This gives a much deeper and fuller sound to many of the chords in the key of D.

Another interesting device is the way modulations are handled. Fairly often the Statlers use an upward change of key to add variety and excitement to a song. By simply sliding the capo to a higher fret (usually one or two frets away) the player only has to learn one chord progression.

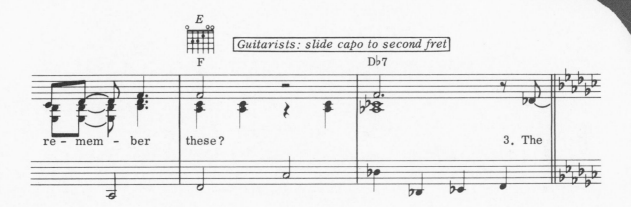

(from "Do You Remember These" Page 32) ✳

How some of the songs were written can provide insight to the nature of the compositions. The Class of '57 was written by Harold and Don Reid within a matter of minutes after watching a television episode of "IRONSIDES" entitled The Class of '57. Do You Know You Are My Sunshine also resulted from a quick process. While performing, the Statlers were asked by a young lady, "do you know You Are My Sunshine?" They thought that was a potentially great title. Several months later they were finishing a recording session for a new album and needed one more song. They remembered the request, and within a few hours had composed the song.

Although enjoyment is the main purpose of this book, we hope that the performance comments and remarks will provide the singer, pianist, and guitarist with a solid introduction to the Statler Brothers' country-gospel style.

Bed Of Roses

Words and Music by
HAROLD REID

Brightly, in 2 (♩ = 1 beat)

She was
She

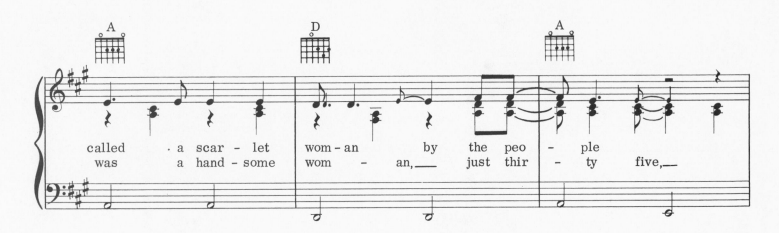

called   a scar-let   wom-an   by the peo - ple
was   a hand-some   wom - an,   just thir - ty five,

Who would go   to church   but left me in the street.
Who was spok - en to   in town by ver - y few.

With no par-ents of   my   own,   I
She man - aged   a late   ev - 'ning

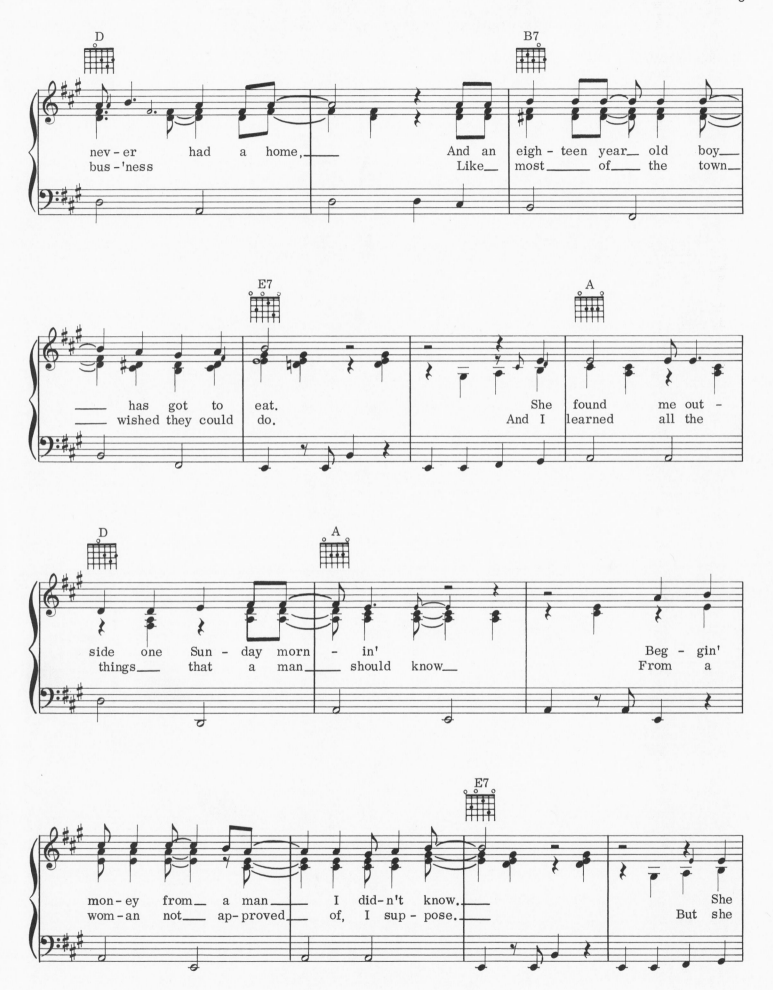

9

Carry Me Back

Words and Music by
DON REID and
HAROLD REID

streets___ of Hol - ly - wood?
wore___ my high school ring?
And
When you

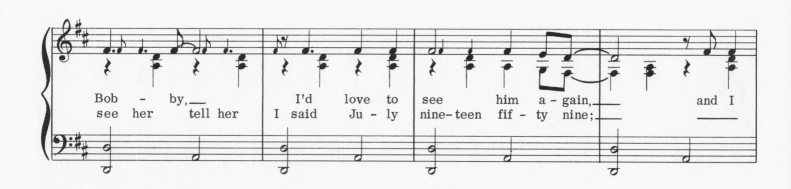

Bob - by,___ I'd love to see him a - gain,___ and I
see her tell her I said Ju - ly nine-teen fif - ty nine;___

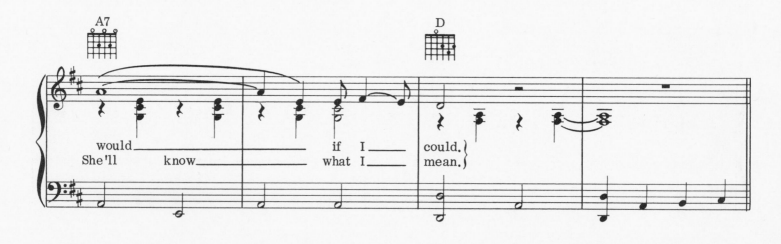

would_____ if I___ could.}
She'll know_____ what I___ mean.}

Chorus

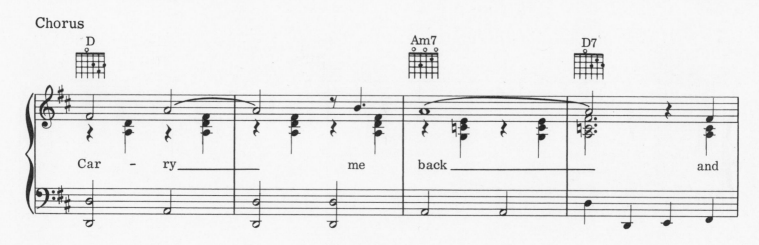

Car - ry_____ me back_____ and

she _____ was al - ways mine.

Car - ry _____ me back, Lord, _____ while

I've _____ still got _ the time. _____

The Class Of '57

Words and Music by
HAROLD REID
and DON REID

may-be we just thought___ the world___ would change to fit our needs.___ The

Class of Fif - ty Sev - en had its dreams.

Guitarists: slide capo to 3rd fret

Guitar → D (Capo on 3rd fret)

Piano → F

Bet-ty runs a trail - er park,
John is___ big in cat - tle,

Jan sells___ tup-per-ware,
Ray is deep___ in debt,

Where

Ran-dy's on an in - sane ward, And
Ma-vis___ fin-'ly wound___ up___

Mar-y's on___ wel - fare,___
is an - y-bod-y's bet,___

Do You Know You Are My Sunshine

Words and Music by
DON REID and
HAROLD REID

In a bright country 2 (♩ = 1 beat)

Chorus

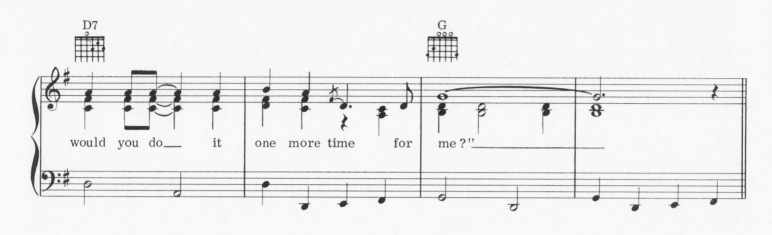

would you do___ it one more time for me?"___

Bor - der to bor - - der and o - cean to o - cean, I
gone just as quick___ as the song that she asked___ for, ___

still look for her ev - 'ry place.___
Tak - ing my sun - shine a - way.___ But

Chas - ing the sun - shine___ each and ev - 'ry night,___ I'm
some - day when I fin - 'lly look___ down___ and see___ her,___ I

Do You Remember These

Words and Music by
DON REID, HAROLD REID
and LARRY LEE

Guitarists: slide capo to 4th fret

Flowers On The Wall

Words and Music by
LEW DeWITT

Note: *This song was recorded ½ step higher in B major. Pianists who wish to play with the record may mentally change the key signature to 5 sharps. Guitarists can capo up 4 instead of 3 frets.*

flow - ers on the wall___ that don't both - er me at all,___

___ Play - in' sol - i - taire___ till

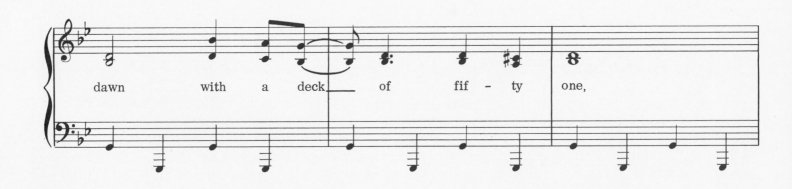

dawn with a deck___ of fif - ty one,

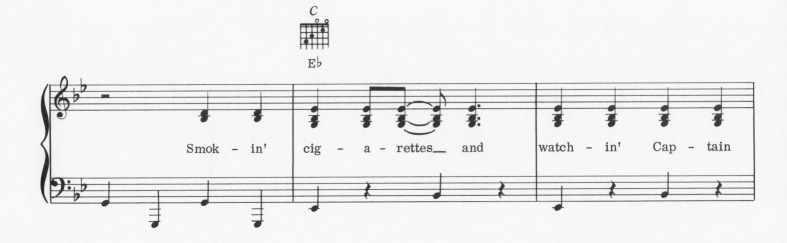

Smok - in' cig - a - rettes___ and watch - in' Cap - tain

I Was There

Words and Music by
DON REID

To Coda ⊕

dig - ni - ty and grace I quiet - ly took my place With the
I ___ loved her first and he ___ loved her worst; I ___
(To Coda)

friends of the bride I was there.
When they

Bridge

had their **first** fight and she called in the night, ___
Though I

know it was - n't right, ___ I ___ was there.
And when

I'll Go To My Grave Loving You

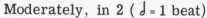

Words and Music by
DON REID

Monday Morning Secretary

Words and Music by
DON REID

Moderately fast, in 2 (♩ = 1 beat)

there bright__ and ear — ly, Mon-day morn — ing sec-re-tar — y, You

Guitarists: slide capo to 3rd fret

sure do__ look pret — ty__ to-day.__

Guitar→D
(Capo on 3rd fret)
Piano→F

At ten__

__ there's a break__ that she don't al-ways take,__ Just

time for— a pow – der— and smoke.   A

sales – man— comes in,—   looks her o – ver end to end,—   And

tells her— a new —————— dirt-y joke.   She

laughs off his pass—   like she's done   in the past,—   She knows—

55

The Movies

Words and Music by
LEW DeWITT

Moderately bright, in 2 (♩ = 1 beat)

New York City

Words and Music by
DON REID

71

Pictures

Words and Music by
LEW DeWITT
and **DON REID**

76

pic-ture that_ we took_ at grad-u - a - tion,_ I'm so

glad you talked_ me out_ of quit-tin' school. Here I

am when I worked at the fill-ing sta - tion,_ And here's

one of Er-nie act - ing like_ a fool._ Here's the

Silver Medals And Sweet Memories

Words and Music by
DON REID

Susan When She Tried

Words and Music by
DON REID

Thank God I've Got You

Words and Music by
DON REID

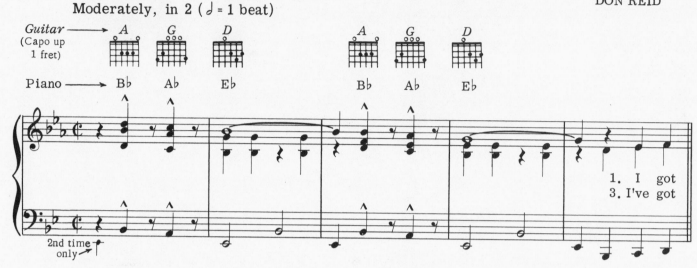

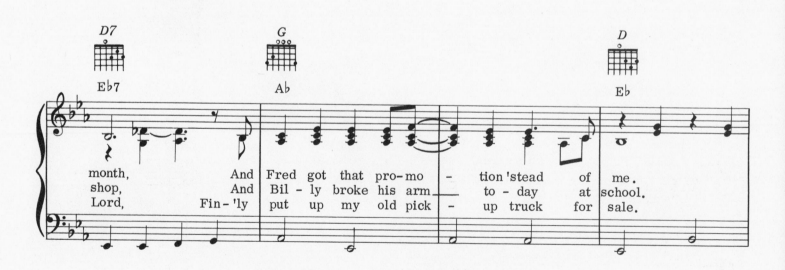

89

Thank You World

Words and Music by
DON REID and
LEW DeWITT

Thank you, world, for let-ting me_ con - trib-ute to_ the cause._

Guitarists: remove capo

Oh, world, you've giv-en

me a place that I_ call_ mine. Tho' I've stepped out of it_

_ and I've got-ten out_ of line,_ Some- times I sing your

Whatever Happened To Randolph Scott

Words and Music by
DON REID and
HAROLD REID

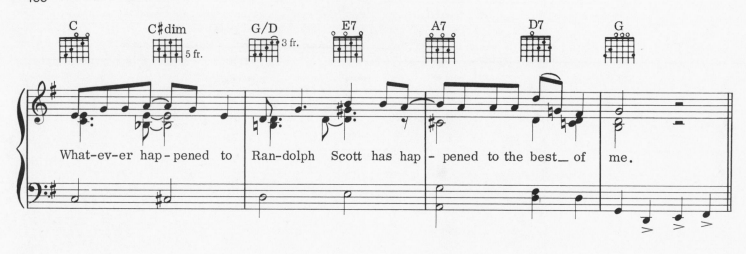

What-ev-er hap-pened to Ran-dolph Scott has hap-pened to the best__ of me.

N.C.

Verse 2

Ev-'ry-bod-y's try-ing to make a com-ment a-bout our doubts and fears. "True

Grit's" the on-ly mov-ie I've real-ly un-der-stood in years.__ You

When You Are Sixty-Five

Words and Music by
DON REID

Guitarists: slide capo to 2nd fret

Who Am I To Say

Words and Music by
KIM REID

Recorded ½ tone higher in A♭; guitarists may capo up one fret.

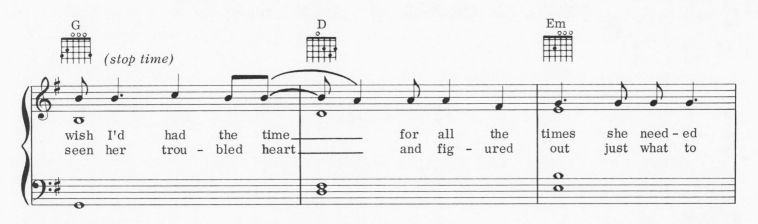

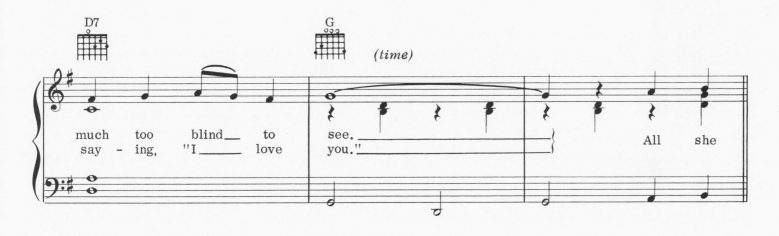

Chorus

Woman Without A Home

Words and Music by
DON REID

Slowly, but with a steady beat

She was young and I was old-er; She be-lieved_____ ev-'ry-thing I told her; She gave her heart and soul___ to me, And more I want-ed. She left home

DISCOGRAPHY

Album	Label
Alive At Johnny Mack Brown High School	Mercury, SRM-1-708
Bed Of Roses	Mercury, SR-61317
The Best Of The Statler Brothers	Mercury, SRM-1-1037
Carry Me Back	Mercury, SRM-1-676
Country America Loves	Mercury, SRM-1-1125
Country Music Then & Now	Mercury, SR-61367
Country Symphonies In E Major	Mercury, SR-61374
Entertainers On & Off The Record	Mercury, SRM-1-5007
Harold, Lew, Phil & Don	Mercury, SRM-1-1077
Holy Bible—New Testament	Mercury, SRM-1-1051
Holy Bible—Old Testament	Mercury, SRM-1-1052
Innerview	Mercury, SR-61358
Pictures Of Moments To Remember	Mercury, SR-61349
Short Stories	Mercury, SRM-1-1173
Sons Of The Motherland	Mercury, SRM-1-1019
The Statler Brothers Sing The Big Hits	Columbia, CS 9519
Thank You World	Mercury, SRM-1-707
The World Of The Statler Brothers	Columbia, CG 31557